Meditate to Thrive

The Dr. Una Academy

603 Old Norcross Rd. Ste A

Lawrenceville, GA 30046

All scripture quotations, unless otherwise indicated, are taken from THE HOLY BIBLE, NEW LIVING TRANSLATION VERSION. NLT.

Copyright© 1996, 2004, 2015, by Tyndale House Publishers, Inc. Carol Stream, Illinois 60188. All rights reserved.

ISBN: 978-0-578-80537-5

Printed in the United States of America.

Meditate to Thrive

The 31 Day Devotional that Makes the Bible Come Alive

Dr. Una

DR. UNA

To Steve.

My husband, closest
friend, and favorite
preacher.

Your mentorship has made
me the woman I am today.

TABLE OF CONTENTS

From the Author

2020 turned out to be an interesting year!

There were so many challenges – a pandemic, financial hardships, and political unrest on a global scale, which triggered fear, worry, and anxiety like I have never seen before.

In the midst of all that, I decided to hold on to the one thing I know never changes – the Word of God.

I decided to study it, not to comply with a religious ritual, but as a manual for everyday life.

This turned out to be one of the most exciting things I have ever done. It gave me faith over fear and peace over anxiety.

I started sharing what I received from my study time in a private Facebook group. By popular demand, the devotional you now hold in your hands was born.

My hope is that you find faith in the One who can keep us and a new love for His Word.

God bless,

Dr. Una

DAY 1

Are you connected?

◆ ◆ ◆

"Yes, I am the vine; you are the branches. Those who remain in me, and I in them, will produce much fruit. For apart from me, you can do nothing."

John 15:5 (NLT)

Jesus used a lot of everyday concepts to teach. I believe He did this so we could understand better.

He is the vine; I am a branch.

Hmm…

The branch is the part of the vine that produces fruit, but the ONLY way it can do so is if it stays CONNECTED.

If the branch is disconnected, it can stay alive for a while, but it won't produce fruit.

In fact, after it dies, it will still exist but only as a dry stick. Kids may play with it or use it for a science project or it may simply be picked up and tossed into the trash.

Either way, once it is disconnected, it will no longer bear fruit.

I guess this is why Jesus said, "Apart from me you can do nothing."

If I want to live a life that bears kingdom fruit like:

- ✅ godly character – joy, peace, love, faithfulness, self-control, etc.
- ✅ living a life of profound impact
- ✅ having my needs met
- ✅ divine health
- ✅ living an enjoyable life

to mention but a few, then I have to stay connected to the vine.

I think if Jesus taught this today, He might have used our cell phones to paint the picture.

Think about the iPhone 11 (Apple fan here – feel free to insert the Samsung Galaxy if that's your thing).

It's a great phone with a lot of capabilities. You can use it to:

- Talk
- Text
- Take pictures
- Create videos
- Manage your calendar
- Check your email
- Stay up-to-date on social media
- Listen to podcasts
- Browse the internet

And the list goes on.

BUT

If the phone is dead, you can do NOTHING.

Nothing, nada, niente, zilch.

Because of this, we do everything in our power to keep our phones charged.

We have chargers at our bedside, in our cars, at work, and just in case, we also keep a mobile power bank.

Well, we are kind of like that iPhone.

We have so many capabilities, but when we aren't charged, we can do nothing.

So how do I stay connected to the vine?

- Prayer
- The Word
- Obedience to the Word.

Three simple but profound disciplines.

If I do not practice these principles, I will gain NOTHING!

I checked up the definition of nothing, and I want nothing to do with it.

Nothing = not anything / no single thing.

Yeah, let's not do that.

I commit to practicing consistent connection.

What do you think about this verse? What are you going to do differently?

Dr. Una

DAY 2

I've got the power

◆ ◆ ◆

As I read the scriptures, I discovered that I'm much more powerful than I thought!

Take a look at what the Word says about us:

> Death and life are in the power of the tongue …
>
> (Proverbs 18:20, KJV)

A simple statement, yet very profound.

Death and life are powerful phenomenons.

But the scriptures don't acknowledge their power – they acknowledge the power of my tongue!

According to that verse, while death and life may seem powerful, the power over them lies in my tongue.

Sounds strange, but not if you take a moment to think about it.

We are made in the image and likeness of God (Genesis 1:26). This means we were made to look and function like God. When He needed to create, from where did He start?

He started by using His Words.

Think about it: The Bible says He came to a place that was "formless and empty and darkness covered the deep waters." (Genesis 1:2 NLT)

I would have said things like:

> "Oh, wow, this place is a mess!"

> "My goodness, it is so dark here."

> "This is a hopeless situation."

He didn't say anything like that at all.

The first words out of His mouth were, "Light, be!"

He didn't say what He saw; He said what He *wanted* to see.

He saw "death" but knew that with His words, He could create life, so He spoke life!

As people made in His image, we also initiate creation in our world by what we say.

What I speak becomes my reality – literally.

The million-dollar question I now need to ask myself is this:

WHAT HAVE I BEEN CREATING WITH MY WORDS?

Life? Death?

What have I been saying about myself, my marriage, future, health, finances, business?

Based on what I have been saying, am I creating life or death?

What do I say when I'm angry, sad, or frustrated?

If I truly believe I will have what I say, would I say what I have been saying over the last few weeks?

Serious stuff, right?

These are my four steps in response to this scripture, and I invite you to join me.

Take an honest inventory of what I have been saying.

Make a quality decision to speak words that produce life.

Make a quality decision to never curse my life by speaking words that produce death in my life.

Spend time in the Word so I can find the right words to speak over every aspect of my life.

What do you think about this verse? What are you going to do differently?

DAY 3

Just for parents

◆ ◆ ◆

I'm a mommy to four wonderful kids.

They are twelve, ten, six, and five, and they are the loves of my life.

I feel a great sense of responsibility toward them all the time.

Am I setting them up to succeed?

Are they getting the right education, building the right skills, cultivating the right relationships?

Am I doing all I can to help them be the best version of themselves AND fulfill God's calling on their lives?

I'm not sure if I will ever know with certainty that I am. I do my best day-to-day and trust God to help me.

In my study today, I found a scripture that gives me some direction:

> *Discipline your children while there is still hope. Otherwise, you will ruin their lives.*
>
> *Provers 19:18 (NLT)*

Hmm…

Now, most times, when we think about discipline, we think of it in negative terms – but look at synonyms of the word "discipline":

Teach, coach, train, drill, indoctrinate.

Nothing negative about that.

My job is to literally be my kids' coach.

I help them develop the disciplines and habits that will make them successful.

Disciplines like:

- Prayer (especially in the Spirit)
- Studying and obeying the Word
- Practicing God's presence
- Generosity
- Morning routines
- Exercise
- Excellence in their school work
- People skills
- Good character (joy, peace, humility, integrity, and the likes)

The list goes on.

I'm a coach, their coach.

Now back to the verse.

> *Discipline your children while there is still hope. Otherwise, you will ruin their lives.*
>
> *Provers 19:18 (NLT)*

There are three main points from this scripture:

1. I need to discipline them.

2. I need to start that process NOW while there is still hope (because a time is coming when I will have less influence over them).

3. If I choose not to discipline them, I am also choosing to ruin their lives.

Today, I am committing to taking up my role as their coach.

I am choosing to make a list of disciplines to start with and help them develop these disciplines.

I am not procrastinating on this one; I start today.

I will have nothing to do with ruining their lives!

What do you think about this verse? What are you going to do differently?

DAY 4

This is the best day of your life!

◆ ◆ ◆

Starting from today, I'm going to look at my days differently.

Today is a day to enjoy, but it also has another equally important value.

It is the raw material of my tomorrow.

It puts me in control of my tomorrow.

How do I know?

I found this gem…

> *Those too lazy to plow in the right season will have no food at the harvest.*
>
> *Proverbs 20:4 (NLT)*

In the past, I would skip over this verse. After all, I'm not a farmer!

But today, I took a more in-depth look.

There are two seasons in life – planting and harvest.

If I am too lazy in the planting season, I will get nothing in the harvest.

If I work hard in the planting season, I will get huge crops in the harvest.

So, what does that mean for me?

Today is the planting season for tomorrow.

I can control what my life will look like a year or five or twenty years from now by what I do with today.

It means if I dream of the future but refuse to take action right now, I am just that: a dreamer.

A 24-hour period is nothing to waste. It is so precious!

So, these are the questions I am asking myself today:

Spiritual – Am I sowing time in prayer and meditation that will produce a deeper walk with God?

Marriage – Am I deliberately doing things today to make my marriage even better tomorrow, or have I slipped into cruise control?

Children – Am I training them in the way they should go? Am I setting them up for a successful future? To fulfill God's calling on their lives?

Legacy – Someday, I'm going to show up before Jesus to tell Him what I did for Him with this wonderful life He gave me. What am I doing today to produce the answer I want to give Him on that day? What am I doing to ensure that I will hear Him say, "Well done, thou good and faithful servant"?

Finances – Am I budgeting, saving, giving, investing in this season of my life to create financial security for myself and an inheritance for my children and their children?

Health – I'm going to be 90 years old someday. What am I doing today to make sure the 90-year-old version of me will be healthy and strong? If I sow the right habits like clean eating and exercise today, I will reap healthy years in the future. Am I doing that?

Personal development – The books I read, podcasts I listen to, and courses and coaching I invest in today create a better life for me tomorrow. Am I investing in my personal development?

I might convince myself that I'm too busy to even think about this or that it's too hard.

And it might be true (well, kinda)…

BUT:

If I truly believe God's Word and know that what I'll see in my future is tied to what I do today, I will make the time, even if it is to do a little bit.

If I know I can't reap what I didn't sow, I'll do the hard work (painful as it is) of sowing now.

I am grateful that I am discovering this now when I am still in the season where I can do something about it.

I am celebrating because I can course correct now.

My commitment?

I will live my days with purpose.

I will enjoy them, have fun, and smell the roses.

AND

I will see the day for what it is.

The seed of tomorrow.

My God-given right to control what my tomorrow will look like.

And I will invest it accordingly.

This is a little heavy, but not as heavy as sitting on the bed of regret in your old age.

It's time to invest!

What do you think about this verse? What are you going to do differently?

_____

_____

_____

_____

_____

_____

_____

_____

_____

_____

_____

_____

_____

_____

_____

_____

DAY 5

Am I a Christian?

◆ ◆ ◆

Somewhere along the line, I subconsciously made "a good person" a synonym for "Christian."

If I met someone at church, he or she was automatically a Christian.

If I met someone at church who was nice, he or she was a very good Christian.

Over the past months, I've been using the book to re-examine my thoughts, and I discovered that this is so far from the truth.

Let's look at where the Bible first mentions the word "Christian."

The disciples were called Christians first at Antioch. Acts 11:26b (NIV)

The name "Christian" was given to disciples – not to people who attended church; not to people who spoke "Christianese," but disciples!

What is a disciple?

Disciple = one who accepts and assists in spreading the doctrines of another. (Merriam-Webster Dictionary)

So Christ's disciple is someone who accepts His teachings (which means they live by them), and also helps others live by His teachings.

No wonder Jesus gave this final instruction to His disciples:

Therefore, go and make disciples of all the nations, baptizing them in the name of the Father and the Son and the Holy Spirit. Teach these new disciples to obey all the commands I have given you... Matthew 28:19-20a (NLT).

Seems like Jesus is very interested in disciples.

No mention of converts or churchgoers, even though these are things that Christians are too.

The name "Christian" was given to disciples. Jesus wants His disciples to adhere to His teachings and teach others to do the same.

So, in reflection, I ask myself...

Am I a Christian?

I could religiously say "yes," or I could dig further to find the truth.

Do I follow His teachings?

Do I even know what His teachings are?

Do I teach others to follow His teachings?

The degree to which I do these things is really the degree to which I am a Christian.

Tough pill to swallow, but I'd rather do that than get a shock in heaven.

So, what is my commitment today?

To become a better Christian!

- ✓ I'll do what it takes to know Him better.

- ✓ I'll read His Word, fully intending to obey.

- ✓ I'll help others develop Christian disciplines.

I think I'll start using the word disciple more too – it really puts it into perspective.

P.S. Please note that the Bible commands church attendance, so I am not in any way saying it is not relevant – it's one of the things disciples do!

What do you think about this verse? What are you going to do differently?

DAY 6

Mirror, mirror on the wall

◆ ◆ ◆

As a young Christian, I was very intrigued by people who walked in great faith. I still am.

These people seemed to be so confident that God would show up.

I mean, how do you lay hands on the sick in front of everyone, knowing that God will heal them?

How do you believe God for prosperity amid a recession? I know His Word said it, but still…

How do you believe God so much for your big dreams that you say it out loud in front of others, knowing full-well that it will come to pass?

I mean, I believed God, too. Kinda…

I had a lot of doubts and questions.

Then I stumbled on scripture I have been practicing for at least two decades now, more so in the last few years:

> But we all, with unveiled face, beholding as in a mirror the glory of the Lord, are being transformed into the same image from glory to glory, just as by the Spirit of the Lord.
>
> 2 Corinthians 3:18 (NKJV)

There are three parts to this thought.

✦ Behold as in a mirror the glory of the Lord.

When the Bible uses the word "image," it is to help us understand.

There are two things I want to show you about the mirror:

First, we use it to figure out how we look. We never argue about the reflection we see in the mirror.

In the same way, when we look into the Word and see things written about us as Christians, we need to accept that as our reflection and stop arguing.

Secondly, most people look in the mirror EVERY DAY.

In the same way, we need to look at His glory daily through the Word and in the place of prayer and worship, both personally and corporately.

✦ Being transformed.

This is the consequence of beholding the mirror daily.

YOU WILL CHANGE!

You will become more like Him in character, faith, creativity, and wisdom.

You will literally become a sign and wonder to your generation.

You don't have control over transformation, but you do have control over looking in the mirror.

The more you do it, the more you are transformed.

📌 From glory to glory

This transformation does not happen once; it happens from one level to another.

This is what used to throw me off.

I wanted to be a firm believer who was very close to God and could do great things for Him all at once.

That's not really how it works.

I start from where I am, behold His glory day by day, and reflect that glory to my world.

As I continue to look in the mirror, I break into a higher level of glory, and then I reflect that to my world.

And this process should continue until either Jesus comes or I go.

True to His Word, I have continually grown.

But guess what I have recommitted to doing?

Beholding as in a mirror the glory of the Lord.

We can become EVERYTHING God has called us to be IF we will go through this process.

Don't be thrown off by the time it takes to "become."

Know that God's Word cannot be broken. He will do what He said.

Rather than focus on BECOMING, focus on BEHOLDING.

If you will behold, you will become!

What do you think about this verse? What are you going to do differently?

_____

_____

_____

_____

_____

_____

_____

_____

_____

_____

_____

_____

_____

_____

_____

_____

_____

_____

_____

_____

_____

DAY 7

Is it really that simple?

◆ ◆ ◆

One of the decisions I made in recent years is to be a doer of the Word; to simply find out what it says and do it.

While reading, I found this scripture:

> Rejoice in the Lord always: and again I say, Rejoice.
>
> Philippians 4:4 KJV

"Rejoice" means to feel or show great joy or delight.

Well, I thought, I am committed to obeying, but what if I am having a bad day?

What if on that day, I experience disappointment or face challenges?

If the Word says to always rejoice, then it means I can – in good times and bad.

So what is there to rejoice about on a bad day?

I pulled up 12 for myself:

😵 I am alive, I am still here, I have another shot.

☺ I am the object of God's affection, the apple of His eyes. (Zechariah 2:8)

☺ I have a relationship with Jesus, the Son of the living God, heir of all of creation.

☺ I have access to the Blood of Jesus, which serves as a hedge of protection around me.

☺ I have access to the Name of Jesus, the Name above every other name, that at the mention of that Name, EVERY knee must bow. (Philippians 2:10-11)

☺ In Christ, I have access to the throne room of God, the most powerful place in the universe. (Ephesians 2:6)

☺ God has a good plan for my life. (Jeremiah 29:11)

☺ I am the temple of the Holy Spirit. I have the Spirit of God: the custodian of all power, wisdom, and creativity, living on inside me.

☺ I have the ability to hear from God. (John 10:27)

☺ I have access to the Word of God, which is His wisdom.

☺ Because of the price Jesus paid, I am heaven-bound.

☺ All things are working for my good – the good, the bad, the ugly. All of it! (Romans 8:26)

The more I meditate on these facts of the Word, the more I rejoice.

My prayer for today:

Lord,

Help me become more aware of the great things you've done in my life.

Before I was saved, I was hellbound, but you made heaven an option for me.

You accepted me into your family; the kindest, coolest, and most powerful family in the universe.

You didn't leave me alone here; you put your Spirit inside me.

I'm never alone, and I have access to wisdom, creativity, and power that I could never have otherwise.

You have good plans for me, and you have given me a guide to lead me on the journey.

There is ALWAYS a reason to rejoice.

Help me to be that kid who ALWAYS does.

In Jesus' Name,

Amen!

Dr. Una

DAY 8

Is Jesus really my Lord?

◆ ◆ ◆

The more I dig into the Word, the more I discover that some things I've thought Christians should be, do, or have are simply not true.

It definitely makes me want to study more because I need to get rid of as many wrong assumptions as possible and replace them with the truth.

Somewhere in the prayer of salvation, we make this statement:

> I accept you (Jesus) as my Lord and Savior.
> If I say Jesus is my Lord, then I have to look at this question He asked some of his followers who said the same thing:
> "So why do you keep calling me 'Lord, Lord!' when you don't do what I say?"

> Luke 4:46 NLT.

37

Jesus seems to expect that if I call Him Lord, I should do what He says.

That means when I read the Word, I read it intending to obey.

That means when I read the Word and what it says is different from my opinion, I drop my opinion and pick up His.

- ✅ Is it possible that He is my savior but not my Lord?
- ✅ Is He Lord in some areas but not others?
- ✅ Do I obey Him in the area of prayer but not in making disciples?
- ✅ Do I obey Him in the area of my relationships with others but not in my finances?

Today is a day for reflection and self-examination.

- Where have I been obedient to His Word?
- Where have I been disobedient to His Word?
- Where have I chosen my opinion over His?

This self-reflection is so important because we are going to answer these questions when we show up on the other side of eternity. We might as well prepare for it.

Today is also a good day to make a quality decision.

Jesus is my LORD and savior!

What do you think about this verse? What are you going to do differently?

DAY 9

God loves me!

◆ ◆ ◆

"For the mountains may move and the hills disappear, but even then my faithful love for your will remain."

Wow!

God does not just love me; He loves me with faithful love.

That sounds amazing, but wait till you see the actual definition of faithful!

Faithful = loyal, constant, steadfast.

So when does God love me?

All the time.

Every single second of every single day.

Unfortunately, we live in a time when the prevailing version of love is what we see in the movies.

'Love' today, hate tomorrow.

'Love' without commitment.

It sometimes makes it difficult to understand the love of God.

The love of God is relentless, extravagant, and so unchanging that I can always count on it.

It is not a feeling; it is a commitment.

My favorite definition of love as a commitment is the sustained direction of will toward the good of another.

That is exactly what God has for me!

To show how constant His love for me is, He gives two word pictures in Isaiah 54:10.

The mountains may move...

I need you to stop and think about this for a moment.

I live in Georgia and have been to the Stone Mountains.

I have traveled to Colorado and seen the breathtaking mountains there.

Imagine a mountain you have seen.

God says that even if the mountains could move, even if something as crazy and dramatic as that happened, His love for me will never change.

Hallelujah!

The hills may disappear...

Hills are not as high as mountains, but they are high.

Imagine sitting with your family at the park, enjoying a fun lunch.

You are at a little restaurant that overlooks a hill, having a great time.

Then, all of a sudden, the hill disappears.

Even if the world changes so much that something as "impossible" as that suddenly becomes possible, God's love will NEVER change.

This is my conclusion.

God loves me with an EVERLASTING, CONSTANT, RELENTLESS LOVE.

I am his beloved.

The apple of His eye.

Never will I believe the lie that He is mad at me and given up on me.

Never will I believe that He is just putting up with me.

He loves me!

What do you think about this verse? What are you going to do differently?

_____

_____

_____

_____

_____

_____

_____

_____

_____

_____

_____

_____

_____

_____

_____

_____

_____

_____

_____

_____

_____

_____

_____

_____

DAY 10

Who's in charge?

◆ ◆ ◆

It's amazing how God uses so many pictures of everyday life to pass across His truths.

It really does make it so much easier to understand.

I guess I should adopt that in my speaking and writing too.

After all, His Book is the bestselling one in the history of the world, with over five billion copies sold as of 2015.

I found this one in my last study:

> "A person without self-control is like a city
> with broken-down walls."
>
> Proverbs 25:28 NLT

So let us examine this a little more closely.

Self-control = the ability to control oneself, in particular one's emotions and desires, or the expression of them in one's behavior, *especially* in difficult situations.

Back in those days, cities had walls around them, primarily for protection from other armies that would try to invade the city.

A city without walls is a city without defense.

Enemies could come in at any time and take over the entire city with all its people and wealth.

Figuratively, this could represent our lives.

We can build the different aspects of our lives – spiritual, family, ministry, finances, and health, but if we do not have self-control, we are vulnerable.

Imagine building a great life and losing it all because of a lack of self-control.

I have to pay close attention to developing the fruit of the Spirit called self-control.

In fact, there is probably no point in building anything else if I won't.

This is a great time to have a come-to-Jesus meeting with myself.

- How do I react when things do not go my way? When someone annoys me? When I'm frustrated? When someone hurts me? When I'm sad?

- Do I lash out, become rude, tantrum, or throw away my Christian values to get back at people who hurt me?

- Am I able to control my desires, or do they control me?

It is so important to tell myself the truth and course-correct as needed.

Fortunately, self-control is one of the fruits of the Spirit listed in Galatians 5:22.

If it is a fruit of the Spirit, it means I already have it.

Now my job is to grow it.

How do things grow?

By feeding and exercise.

I grow in the fruit of the Spirit by feeding (studying the Word about it) and exercising (practicing when situations that challenge my ability to control myself appear).

Today, I make the commitment to do just that.

What do you think about this verse? What are you going to do differently?

_____

_____

_____

_____

_____

_____

_____

_____

_____

_____

_____

_____

_____

DAY 11

The Christian Disadvantage

◆ ◆ ◆

Sometimes, I think we have a "disadvantage" as Christians.

See, the unsaved are very clear that to get results, they would have to do a lot.

They are very clear on the connection between actions and results.

On the other hand, we have God.

A loving Father who:

- ✓ has given us many promises of a preferred future we can stand on.

- ✓ is always willing to help.

- ✓ has given us grace we can lean on in times of need.

- ✓ loves us so much that He gave us His only Son, which is proof that He won't hold anything back.

This is really great, but sometimes we misinterpret it to mean that He will do everything.

We find ourselves no longer correlating action with results.

That's why we have statements like, "God will do it," which is true, but He will do it in partnership with us.

Paul articulated this concept so eloquently:

> But by the grace of God I am what I am, and His grace toward me was not in vain; but I labored more abundantly than they all, yet not I, but the grace of God *which was* with me.
>
> 1 Corinthians 15:10 (NKJV)

Let us dig into this a little more:

Paul was made by grace.

That grace was not in vain (which means the grace of God can be in vain in a person's life).

It was not in vain because he added hard work to it.

He worked hard by grace, not just his power and might.

Working with God's grace = labor, working without grace / toiling.

Time to look inwards.

My life has so many areas.

- 🎯 My walk with God
- 🎯 Marriage, kids
- 🎯 Ministry
- 🎯 Health
- 🎯 Finances
- 🎯 Business/Career

🎯 Personal development

Am I doing my part?

The more I release my faith for God's grace (the super), and the more I do my part (natural), the more of the SUPERNATURAL I will see in my life.

There is a reason why the Holy Spirit is called our helper, not our doer.

We do the doing; He does the helping.

There is also a reason why the Bible says faith without work is dead. When we don't add work, we literally abort our faith's results.

Today is a great day for prayer and commitment.

Prayer: Lord, I pray that you open my eyes to see the areas where my lack of action limits your grace's impact in my life.

Commitment: I make a commitment not to allow the grace you put on my life to be in vain. Amen!

What do you think about this verse? What are you going to do differently?

DAY 12

I'm a masterpiece

◆ ◆ ◆

Sometimes when I read the scriptures, I just want to SCREAM because it is just so good.

Today was one of those days.

Look at this verse:

> For we are God's masterpiece. He has created us anew in Christ Jesus, so we can do the good things he planned for us long ago.
>
> Ephesians 2:10 (NLT).

Now, let's unpack this.

Truth #1

I am God's masterpiece!

A masterpiece is a work of outstanding artistry, skill, or workmanship.

That's who I am!

Not ordinary, not a nobody, not mediocre, not average – a masterpiece.

Not the masterpiece of a regular artist or even a genius like Picasso, but a masterpiece of the entire universe's creator.

The One who made the beautiful turquoise waters of Turks and Caicos, the picturesque mountains of Colorado, and all the human body's intricate details.

Yeah, that same One. I'm His masterpiece.

I'm pretty special!

Truth #2

I was created anew!

When I accepted Jesus as my Lord and savior, I was made brand new. (Also 2 Corinth. 5:17).

Brand new!

Not refurbished, not renovated, but brand new.

That means I need to stop looking at my past to determine what my life can look like now.

That means I need to stop thinking how I used to because life is different now.

Think about how much Kate Middleton's life changed because she "accepted" Prince William into her life.

If her life could alter that much because she married a prince, how much more is there of me, now that I'm in partnership with the king of all kings?

I'm brand new in Christ.

Truth #3

I'm on assignment!

I didn't show up on this earth by accident.

I'm not designed to just live and die.

He planned a long time ago good works for me to do.

I wasn't just saved to escape to heaven; I was saved to serve my world.

I'm on assignment.

This leaves me with one train of thought:

Something dramatic happened when I was saved; I was completely recreated.

This new version of me is a masterpiece on assignment.

My commitments today?

Keep studying the Word to find out more about who I am in Christ and my assignment.

Believe what He says about me.

I really want to become EVERYTHING Jesus died to make me.

What do you think about this verse? What are you going to do differently?

DAY 13

The key to transformation

◆ ◆ ◆

I used to think I was static.

"I'm not good at speaking."

"I can't pray like that prayer warrior."

"I don't have faith like that other believer to make the promises of God become my reality."

And the list went on.

BUT…

Thank God we are not static.

I can be one way today, and on purpose, change my life and become better.

Doing this is not a mystery; there is an actual formula to create transformation in our lives.

Be ye transformed by the renewing of your mind.

Romans 12:2 (KJV).

> My spirit is not the problem. I got a brand-
> new one when I got saved.
>
> (2 Corinthians 5:17)

My mind, however, is the same old mind, thinking the same old thoughts.

> This is a HUGE problem because, "As a
> man thinketh, so is he."
>
> (Proverbs 23:7 KJV)

If my thoughts don't change, my life doesn't change.

I can't rise above my thoughts, which means I really need to pay attention to what I think.

So, what do we need to do?

Examine our thoughts. Understand that you don't have to think all the thoughts that come to mind. Some of them are yours, some from satan, and some from God. Using the Word of God as a filter, you can split thoughts into Word-compliant and not Word-complaint. The Bible actually gives a succinct version of a filter you can use to categorize your thoughts in Philippians 4:8. This is critical because our lives move in the direction of our thoughts, so we simply cannot be undisciplined in our thinking.

Reject all thoughts that are not Word-compliant. How? Simple – when a thought comes that does not line up with the Word, open up your mouth and say what the Word says about that same situation. You cannot say one thing and think something else at the same time. Think about when Jesus was tempted. Every time Satan said something that was not Word-compliant, Jesus answered him with the Word. Every single time! He did not keep quiet, and neither should we.

Intentionally think about what the Word says. What does He say about your peace? Your health? Your family? Your finances? Your destiny? His favor on your life? Knowing what He says and adopting that as your new mindset changes EVERYTHING.

You can change, and so can your circumstances, but it all starts with renewing your mind.

The raw material for renewing the mind is the Word of God – not our circumstances, others' experiences, popular opinion, or even our own opinions, but the Word.

Imagine a life that mirrors God's plan for you.

This is a lifelong journey, but there is no better time to start or recommit to it than today.

Who's in?

DAY 14

By their fruits...

◆ ◆ ◆

Sometimes when I study the Word, I get the really yummy stuff, and other times I get spinach.

Spinach is good for me, but I don't particularly care for the taste.

Today, I would have liked a study on how much God loves me, but instead, I got a study on how to know if I'm wise or a fool.

#SpinachWord

The truth is, just like our natural children, we need a balanced diet. And because God is a great Father, He makes sure we get it.

So, here goes:

> A fool is quick-tempered but a wise person
> stays calm when insulted.
>
> Proverbs 12:16 NLT

The thing is, we don't get to choose if we are foolish or wise.

What we get to choose is our actions, and our actions determine if we are foolish or wise.

So, this brings us to a come-to-Jesus moment when we look inward and ask the question…

"Am I quick-tempered?"

"Do I get angry very easily?"

"Do I lose it as soon as I am insulted?"

If my answer to any of these is "yes," then the truth is that I'm surely acting like a fool. (Yikes!)

There could be several reactions to this:

I can decide I disagree with what the Word says.

I can become depressed because I've been acting like a fool.

OR I can course-correct and start acting like a wise person, beginning right now.

My choice?

#3 all day, every day.

(FYI - Notice the scriptures don't say not to respond to things or become a doormat. This is a recommendation on the attitude to have while you respond).

So, how do I become an even-tempered person? How do I stay calm when insulted?

Practice, practice, practice!

If you were about to go off on someone and your ten-year-old daughter and three of her friends walk in, you'd find that you were able to control yourself more than you thought.

If you were up for promotion as president of a company and someone insulted you while a TV crew was there to do an interview, chances are, you would keep it together.

So, maybe we have more control than we think.

Every time we practice, it becomes a little easier.

It is literally like doing reps during a workout.

Every time I practice staying calm when insulted, my "calm" muscle grows, and my "quick-temper" muscle atrophies!

The "workout" will hurt like crazy initially, but it will get easier and easier until it becomes second nature.

All right then – time to start doing my "wisdom workouts"!

What do you think about this verse? What are you going to do differently?

P.S. thanks for sharing my spinach with me today.

DAY 15

Victory over storms

◆ ◆ ◆

I used to believe that Christians have a picture-perfect life with no storms because God takes care of all that.

Then, as I read through the Book of Isaiah, I found this verse:

When you go through deep waters,

> I will be with you.

When you go through rivers of difficulty,

> you will not drown.

When you walk through the fire of oppression,

> you will not be burned up;

> the flames will not consume you.

Isaiah 43:2 NLT

There is no "if" to it – we WILL experience storms.

The difference for Christians is that we won't need to face them alone. He will be right there with us, and He will make sure we weather the storm and come out on top!

So the question is, what do I need to do to position myself to be the kind of person storms cannot stop?

I saw a three-part sequence Jesus gave, so let us take a look:

> I will show you what it's like when someone <u>comes to me, listens to my teaching, and then follows it.</u> It is like a person building a house who digs deep and lays the foundation on solid rock. When the floodwaters rise and break against that house, it stands firm because it is well built.
>
> Luke 6:47-48 NLT

It seems simple, but this step is critical. Am I casual about my relationship with Him, or do I treat Him as the source of everything? Do I spend time with Him when it's convenient, or have I made it a daily non-negotiable in my life? Do I lean on Him, or do I lean on me? Have I come to Him?

Listen to my teaching – the day of a storm is not the best time to start listening to His teaching. This is something we cultivate as a habit, knowing that He knows what is coming, and He will make sure we are prepared for it.

Follow it – listening with the intention to obey creates victory!

According to Jesus, if I do all three, I will be immune to the storms' detrimental impact.

What does this look like in everyday life?

Making a commitment to a few non-negotiables.

Prayer – If I know I can't predict when storms will come, AND I don't have what it takes to overcome them, then

I need to depend on Jesus daily. I need to show up every day to spend time talking to Him and hearing Him talk back. The best thing is to schedule your prayer time every day – almost like a daily date with Jesus. Start from whatever length of time you can do consistently, then work on increasing it. Have an ever-changing schedule? No problem. When you get your work agenda, schedule your Jesus dates. The bottom line is that this must be done.

Study – The strategies of success and stories of how others did it that will grow your faith are found in the scriptures. Do all you can to be a student of the Word; it is truly life-changing. This is the primary vehicle for building faith, and it is by our faith that we overcome. It could be a Bible-in-a-year plan, a chapter a day, a topical study, and so on. If you commit to putting the Word in you daily, then the dramatic transformation in your life will shock you.

Obey – This is the not-so-fun part, but it yields very high dividends. As you read, obey. As you discover the things Jesus taught that you are not doing, start doing them. If there are things He says His disciples shouldn't do, stop them. Spoiler alert – the Bible will call you out *a lot*, but it is for your own good.

These are not exciting or profound; they are just three simple things.

BUT…

They are the three powerful things that set you up to have victory over storms.

What do you think about this verse? What are you going to do differently?

DAY 16

It's my turn

◆　◆　◆

Imagine a brand-new muscle car like a Ferrari.

It has amazing acceleration, going from 0-62 mph in a mind-blowing 2.9 seconds and a top speed of 211mph!

What if that car was totaled in an accident and a master mechanic decided to restore it?

Of course, he could restore it and make it pretty much brand-new again; they are geniuses, after all.

He could put in a brand-new engine, one that could make the car go from 0-62 mph again.

He could work on the body, and it would look like it had never been in an accident.

What if he did all that but didn't change the tires?

Think about it – you would have a powerful car with 12 cylinders and 789 horsepower.

You would have a beautiful car, one people would love to pose on while taking social media-worthy selfies.

But you would have a car that will be GROUNDED because it has no tires.

How frustrating!

The lack of functional tires will make a car with such power completely useless.

I said all that to say: when you are saved, you get a brand-new "engine," which is your spirit – that's God's part.

God is not in the business of changing your "tires," which is your mind – that's your part.

The dangerous thing about our responsibility is that if we don't do it, we ground the "car."

We ground our ability to express the DRAMATIC change that happened to us when we became Christians.

Look at what God says in His Word:

> *Do not conform to the pattern of this world, but be transformed by the renewing of your mind.*
>
> *Romans 12:2a NIV*

You are saved, yes, but how do you bring about transformation in your character, family, health, finances, and the legacy you leave in your world?

By renewing your mind.

What is the raw material for transforming your mind?

The Word of God.

> ✦ If you think the same way you did before you came to Christ, your life will stay the same, even though you have a brand new engine.

★ If you think the same way, you will limit God's ability to intervene in your life even though you are the literal temple of God (1 Corinthians 6:9), carrying Him around everywhere you go.

God paid the ultimate price by sending His only Son to die for us.

We must pay the ultimate price by completely transforming our minds.

How?

✓ Staying in the Word with humility, adopting God's way of thinking as ours.

✓ Staying in the Word and using it to search out mind "viruses" (ways of thinking that are different from God's) and removing them.

✓ Staying in the Word with the intention to obey.

If we do this, our lives will be like the Ferrari that was once grounded but now has brand-new tires.

#FastCar #LeftInTheDust

I am committed to spending time daily changing my mind.

I will adopt God's way of thinking as mine.

My era of arguing with the Word of God is OVER.

I'm not going to stay grounded!

What do you think about this verse? What are you going to do differently?

DAY 17

Well, there goes my excuse

◆　◆　◆

Like everyone else, I have "good reasons" why I can't do certain things.

I mean, as a busy doctor who is also a wife, mom of four, and serial entrepreneur, there are many times when I can "legitimately" say I don't have time for certain disciplines, like studying the Word, prayer, and investing in other people's lives.

"Even God understands," I would think to myself.

Then I stumbled on this scripture:

> *Before daybreak the next morning, Jesus got up and went out to an isolated place to pray.*
> *Mark 1:35 NLT.*

Nice!

Jesus prayed early in the morning, a good habit.

That's what I thought, but I didn't fully understand the implication of that verse until I read about the kind of day he had before that morning.

Jesus had a day similar to a 24-hour call before that morning.

Let's take a look.

⚔ The synagogue, Mark 1:21-27

He went with His disciples to the synagogue and taught a full sermon. While there, a demon-possessed man started manifesting, and Jesus cast out the devil.

⚔ Peter's home, 1 Mark 1:29-31

After teaching at the synagogue, they went to Peter's home. His mother-in-law was sick with a fever, and Jesus healed her. After that, they had dinner.

⚔ Peter's home, 2 Mark 1:32-34

Imagine that after a day like the one He had, many sick and demon-possessed people were brought to Peter's house. So a whole new healing service started, and the WHOLE town was there to watch! The funny thing is, the Bible actually says this second part started "that evening after sunset…".

Hmm…

So when did it end?

I would say that it was a hectic day.

Personally, I would have thought about skipping prayer, studying the Torah, and preaching to others for a few days. (Shhh …don't tell!)

Now that we've looked at the pretext, let's reread our key scripture:

> *Before daybreak the next morning, Jesus got up and went out to an isolated place to pray.*
>
> Mark 1:35 NLT.

After all that, He still got up before daybreak to pray!

That tells me a few things:

1. Jesus placed a high premium on prayer.
2. Jesus had a daily habit of praying. (I think this because if any day was a great one to skip it, it was that day. If He didn't, then He probably never did).

I no longer have any excuses.

So what does that mean for me?

I have to decide that prayer is non-negotiable.

Once I make that decision, all my creative juices go into motion to help me figure out how to get it done.

And I'll be so much better for it.

What do you think about this verse? What are you going to do differently?

Dr. Una

DAY 18

Love in the air

◆ ◆ ◆

It turns out this love thing is very serious!

Look at this…

> "Your love for one another will prove to the world that you are my disciples."
>
> John 13:35 (NLT)

The proof that I am a disciple is my love for others – not making other disciples, not teaching powerfully, not performing miracles, but loving others!

So, let's unpack God's thoughts about what love is – well, a small portion of it.

Love is patient and kind. 1 Corinthians 13:4a (NLT)

When I first read that verse, I felt I wasn't doing too badly.

I mean, I'm kinda patient and kind.

When I looked up the dictionary meaning of both words, though, I realized I have work to do.

Kind = having or showing a friendly, generous, and considerate nature.

Patience = the capacity to accept or tolerate delay, trouble, or suffering without getting angry or upset.

Without getting angry or upset?

Let's bring this to everyday life. If I love people, it means:

- when people create delays (including driving a little slower in traffic), I don't get upset or angry.

- when things are not going my way in a relationship, I don't get upset or angry.

- when people don't change (habits, character flaws, etc.) as fast as I want them to, I don't get upset or angry.

Yikes!

Well, I said yikes, then I remembered who I am.

I am a Christian!

When I got saved, I became a brand-new person. (2 Corinthians 5:17)

A brand-new person who has the capacity to love!

Look at what the scriptures say about us:

> And hope does not put us to shame, because *God's love has been poured out into our hearts through the Holy Spirit, who has been given to us.*
>
> Romans 5:5 (NIV)

Notice that "poured" is in the past tense.

A deposit of the love of God has already been made in my heart!

So no excuses here; I already have the "love muscle" in my heart.

If I am not patient, it is because the love muscle is flabby from poor nutrition (not feeding on the Word about love), and lack of use (not practicing when opportunities to love arise), but I *can* develop bodybuilder-type muscles.

> So, how do I become great at loving?

> How do I become a person who does not get angry or upset easily?

> How do I become a generous, considerate person?

By developing my love muscle with proper nutrition and exercise.

Starting today, I'm enrolling in the love gym!

What do you think about this verse? What are you going to do differently?

Dr. Una

DAY 19

Sunrise in Jamaica

◆ ◆ ◆

Two years ago, I had the privilege of going to Jamaica.

(P.S. If you're Jamaican, just know that I love you and your country!)

Knowing I absolutely LOVE the ocean, my husband got us a room with a balcony overlooking it.

It was such a BEAUTIFUL view.

After looking at the room, I asked my husband for one thing: I wanted to have the balcony to myself every morning for my devotion time.

I imagined praying and studying, overlooking the ocean and watching the sunrise over the horizon!

The next morning while it was still a little dark, I made my way to the balcony and worshipped.

Then the sun started rising.

Initially, it was just like a yellow dot over the ocean, and then it became brighter and brighter until all the darkness was gone.

It was glorious!

Arguably the most beautiful sunrise I have ever seen.

It gave a certain scripture I had always quoted a whole new meaning:

> The path of the righteous is like the morning sun, shining ever brighter till the full light of day.
>
> Proverbs 4:18 (NIV)

The Word likens my life to the same beautiful sunrise I saw.

What? Yes!

The plan is for my life to get better and better until the day He comes, or I go to be with Him.

Does this mean I will never face difficulties? No.

What it does mean is that difficulties cannot stop me.

We face difficulties every day – from little things like dragging ourselves out of bed when we really want to sleep and staying sane in rush-hour traffic to more challenging issues like working out relationship problems. We don't let difficulties stop us. Instead, we continue to make progress despite them.

So, what does this mean for me?

- ✅ I can have a different outlook on life!
- ✅ I can believe what the Word says and that my life is getting better day-by-day.
- ✅ I can believe that my life in God is designed in a way that my relationship with God gets deeper day-by-day, my character becomes more Chr,ist-like, and I become better at deploying my faith to make God's promises my reality!

That's the way my life is supposed to be.

So what is my part to play? Remember that faith without work is dead.

I take action!

- What do I need to do to experience a deeper walk with God?

Spend time in prayer and the Word.

- What do I need to do to have a more Christ-like character?

Study and practice Christ-like characters. Just like in any sport, practice hurts, but the rewards are AMAZING!

- What do I need to do to make the promises in the Bible my reality?

Find them in the Bible, believe them, start declaring them, and take the corresponding actions.

> The path of the righteous is like the morning sun, shining ever brighter till the full light of day.
>
> Proverbs 4:18 (NIV)

Such a beautiful scripture.

If I believe this, it will be so much easier to believe that "all things are working for my good," according to Romans 8:28.

All things - the good, bad, and ugly, are working to make my light shine brighter and brighter!

I know there have been unique challenges this year, but I want to invite you to get your hopes up.

God's Word, promises, and good plans for your life haven't changed.

He is calling you to spend time with Him; believe what His Word says, and take bold action.

He is with you, and He will fight for you!

There are so many days left in your life, and with Him, you can create a masterpiece. I am committed to doing just that.

What do you think about this verse? What are you going to do differently?

_____

_____

_____

_____

_____

_____

_____

_____

_____

_____

_____

_____

_____

_____

_____

_____

DAY 20

My strategy for
a great year

◆ ◆ ◆

A new year is about to roll in, and I wonder what the best way to spend the days left in this year is.

I want next year to be my best year yet, but I have been alive long enough to know that for that to happen, I have a part to play.

After thinking about it and waiting on God, this is what I came up with:

GROWTH.

I have to grow.

I am limited to the blessings, experiences, and results that I have the capacity to handle based on my level of growth.

I have a ten-year-old son whom I love very much.

I love him enough to buy him a 2021 Range Rover Vogue, but I won't.

My love for him and my ability to buy him the car are not the issue, it's that he isn't mature enough to handle it!

The sobering question is: What are the things God loves me enough to give me and can afford to give me but won't because I can't handle it yet?

Ouch!

Happy "ouch," but still "ouch."

The scriptures talk about this in an even more eye-opening way.

> *Think of it this way. If a father dies and leaves an inheritance for his young children, those children are not much better off than slaves until they grow up, even though they actually own everything their father had.*
>
> Galatians 4:1 NLT

Think about that.

The Son, the heir to everything, is not much better off than a slave!

What changes everything?

GROWTH.

Okay. Got it – growth.

In what areas do I need to grow?

Well, there's a scripture for that, too:

> And Jesus grew in wisdom and stature, and in favor with God and man.
>
> Luke 2:52 (NIV)

Wisdom – the ability to apply the knowledge learned to daily life. I grow in this area by studying AND practicing the Word.

Stature – referring to health. Make no mistake; He was fit. The walk from Capernaum to Jerusalem was a four-day walk, each day being between 8-12 miles. I grow in this area by watching what I eat and exercising.

Favor with God – referring to a great relationship with God. I grow in this by maintaining a consistent prayer life and obeying Him (as opposed to lip service).

Favor with man – I grow in this by practicing walking in love according to 1 Corinthians 13:4-8. I also have to release my faith for the kind of tribe I want and start going after them. If Jesus needed people to fulfill His destiny, it would be silly of me to think I don't!

I have lots of growing to do!

So, I am going to spend the days left in this year GROWING!

The result will be that I will finish this year strong, and I will lay the foundation for a new year beyond my wildest dreams.

What do you think about this verse? What are you going to do differently?

DAY 21

What do you see?

◆ ◆ ◆

One day in church, my pastor (aka my husband) helped me see the power of perception as I had never seen before.

The church walls were all painted white, and he had us take a long hard look at it.

"What color is it?" he asked.

"White," we all answered.

He then handed out glasses with colored lenses to the entire congregation.

About half of us received red-colored lenses, while the others had blue.

"Now, take another look at the walls. What color are they?"

Not one person said white!

People saw the walls as either red or blue based on the lenses they had.

Even though the wall was white, that wasn't the people's reality.

This brought me to a crazy but true realization:

You do not see things the way they are; you see them the way you think they are, based on your perception.

Your perception colors everything!

This makes the scripture, "As a man thinketh in his heart, so is he," come alive.

As I took this in, it occurred to me how DEADLY a wrong perception is.

In the past, I never created my perception on purpose. This was before I became a student of the Word.

I picked up my perception from my family, circumstances, past experiences, and failures.

The sad fact is that things that grow by default are usually not the ones we want, like weeds.

Similarly, a perception created by default is usually not positive or full of faith.

A great time for a come-to-Jesus moment.

What is my perception of:

- ✅ The availability of God's help in challenging times like now?
- ✅ God's willingness to provide for me?
- ✅ The kind of marriage I can have?
- ✅ The kind of impact I can have in my generation?
- ✅ My ability to change my character flaws?
- ✅ The possibility of having a deep, intimate relationship with God?

✓ Health and longevity?

This list is endless.

I must realize that what I passionately believe about these things might be wrong! #HumbleThoughts

The fact that I've always thought them does not mean they are right. I need to re-evaluate my thoughts in light of God's Word.

I must be humble enough to search the scriptures to find out what God says about these things so I can put on His "glasses."

The most dangerous thing I can do is say, "I know the Word of God says that, BUT what I think is…"

That is just like me fighting to keep my "red glasses" on. As long as I do, I will NEVER see reality, which is the beautiful "white wall." #SelfDeception

Today is a great day to make a commitment and pray.

Here is my prayer; you can tweak it and make it yours.

Lord, I commit to study your Word.

If my thoughts don't line up with your Word, I will replace them with yours so that I can see things as they really are.

I ask for your help.

You know the areas of my life where I have my "red glasses" on.

Point these out to me as I study, talk with other believers, and hear the Word at church.

Give me the grace to diligently change what I think as you expose the deception.

To live a life that mirrors your plan, I have to think your thoughts.

Help me do just that.

I love you, Lord. Becoming your daughter is the best thing that has ever happened to me.

Nneka

Rooting for us, we got this!

What do you think about this verse? What are you going to do differently?

_____

_____

_____

_____

_____

_____

_____

_____

_____

_____

_____

_____

_____

_____

DAY 22

Stop letting your friends choose you!

◆　◆　◆

I still get amazed every time it dawns on me again that I cannot really choose my results.

I choose my actions, and the results are almost guaranteed based on the action I chose.

For instance, look at this beauty:

> Don't befriend angry people or associate with hot-tempered people, or you will learn to be like them and endanger your soul.
>
> Proverbs 22:24-25 (NLT)

Think about it for a second.

It implies that you can't really choose whether or not you will be a hot-tempered person.

Your power of choice only applies to the friendships you have.

If you choose hot-tempered friends, you will learn to be hot-tempered.

If you choose friends who stay calm even when irritating and difficult people provoke them, you will learn to be just like them.

Hmm….

The bottom line is, you will become like the people you spend the most time with.

You choose your friends; they choose what your life will look like.

So, the million-dollar question is, who are my closest friends?

- ✓ What do their lives look like now?
- ✓ What are their character flaws?
- ✓ What are their dreams and goals?
- ✓ What is their attitude toward things that are important to me? Like their relationship with God, family, and the pursuit of a preferred future?
- ✓ If I ended up with a life just like theirs, would I be happy with it?

These questions have to be answered honestly.

Now, does that mean you start looking for perfect people to be friends with?

Nah!

Your only options are imperfect people.

However, some imperfect people make progress toward perfection, while others are stagnant or become worse.

I advise you to pick the former!

So, if I end up looking like my closest relationships, what must I then do?

1. Examine my current relationships – I can do this using the questions we just discussed above.

2. Subtract negative relationships – The friends with vices I don't want need to go. Now, "need to go" may not mean I never talk to them again; it may mean I drastically reduce the time we spend together. Maybe they go from being in my core group of friends to being more of an acquaintance. Hard pill to swallow for sure, but am I going to sacrifice my destiny on the altar of sentiments? (Ouch – that's painful but true).

3. Add positive relationships – I can strategically build my core group of friends. If I see people who chase after God, prioritize family and legacy, and grow day-by-day into the person God called them to be, then you best believe I will add them to my circle. You can create your own positive peer pressure by the people you intentionally add to your group of friends.

This seems so business-like, but it has to be done if you want to become everything God has called you to be.

You won't let your kid be friends with just anyone; you help them choose because you know their friends will influence them.

We are not different just because we are adults.

I am going to take a strategic look at my relationships today and modify them as needed.

I know it is not easy, so I will be praying and rooting for you. #WeGotThis

What do you think about this verse? What are you going to do differently?

_____

_____

_____

_____

_____

_____

_____

_____

_____

_____

_____

_____

_____

_____

_____

_____

_____

_____

_____

_____

DAY 23

Practice with the lions

◆ ◆ ◆

One of my favorite stories in the Bible is that of David and Goliath.

There are so many nuggets in it that I could probably write a whole book!

If you take the time to play out the scene in your mind, you will see why everyone, including Saul, thought David was a little crazy.

The following is a description of Goliath.

He was over nine feet tall! To put this into perspective, the average basketball player in the 2019-2020 season was six foot nine inches tall. Goliath was almost three feet taller!

His armor weighed 125 pounds. I would not be shocked if David weighed just a little more than Goliath's armor!

The tip of his spear (just the tip) weighed fifteen pounds – that's the same as a set of twins weighing seven pounds eight ounces each! And that was just the tip!

Read 1 Samuel 17: 4-7 (NLT).

The thought of fighting him was so scary that the king of Israel and the entire Israeli army ran away.

BUT…

Here comes David.

I don't know how old he was, but he was described as a "youth," so at least I can say he was young.

David sees Goliath, and his reaction was not fear.

He starts asking what will be done for the man who rids Israel of the pagan Philistine who defied the living God's army.

What in the world made him think he could take care of Goliath?

In fact, when he spoke to Saul about his plans, Saul actually said, "Don't be ridiculous!" 1 Samuel 17:32 (NLT)

What was David's secret?

There are so many secrets you can unpack from the story, but let's look at one.

When Saul told him not to be ridiculous, this was his answer:

> *"But David persisted. "I have been taking care of my father's sheep and goats," he said. "When a lion or a bear comes to steal a lamb from the flock, I go after it with a club and rescue the lamb from its mouth. If the animal turns on me, I catch it by the jaw and club it to death. I have done this to both lions and bears, and I'll do it to this pagan Philistine, too, for he has defied the armies of the living*

> *God! The Lord who rescued me from the claws
> of the lion and the bear will rescue me from
> this Philistine!"*
> *Saul finally consented. "All right, go ahead,"
> he said. "And may the Lord be with you!"*
>
> I Samuel 17:34-37 (NLT)

David had been practicing!

The sheep were not his; they belonged to his father.

When the lions and bears showed up, he could have run away, but he didn't.

He fought and rescued the lamb, and if the lion or bear tried to hurt him, he killed them.

Notice the scripture said lions and bears, plural, not *lion* and *bear*.

How many times did he do that?

Over time, he learned how to fight in faith.

I say this because he said, "*The Lord who rescued me from the claws of the lion and the bear…*"

He also learned to fight in partnership. He did his part, and he trusted God to guarantee the victory.

He had practiced fighting with "giants" for so long that when Goliath showed up, he said, "God and I have got this!"

Wow!

What does this mean for me?

It means that the challenges I face today should be seen as training opportunities!

Nothing but opportunities to grow my faith muscles.

- ✈ If there is a contention at work, I can practice activating God's favor on my life that will turn everything around.

- ✈ If I feel pain in my body, I can practice activating God's healing power.

- ✈ If I feel a wave of worry, sadness, frustration, or overwhelm coming on, I can practice activating the Lord's joy.

- ✈ If I have a financial need, I can practice releasing my faith to have my needs met.

- ✈ If my child is struggling in school, I can practice activating supernatural help, just like Daniel had in his life (Daniel 1:17,20).

When I see challenges, they should look like a ten-pound weight that I can lift to build muscle.

That way, when "Goliath" shows up, I will rise to the occasion and take him out.

I'm officially enrolling in The Challenges gym. Care to join me?

What do you think about this verse? What are you going to do differently?

DAY 24

What do you want me to do for you?

◆ ◆ ◆

This sounds like a great question, like a blank check.

Well, at least until you understand the context.

This was a question Jesus asked a man who was OBVIOUSLY blind. I mean, he was even called "Blind" Bartimaeus; that's how much his blindness defined him.

Jesus was in his area with a huge crowd following him as usual. The second that Blind Bartimaeus heard about it, he started screaming at the top of his lungs, "Jesus, Son of David, have mercy on me!"

He screamed so much that many in the crowd started shouting at him to be quiet.

Apparently, he didn't care much about what the people thought because the Bible says he shouted even louder!

Finally, he got Jesus's attention, who sent for him.

"What do you want me to do for you?"

Erm, Jesus, EVERYONE can see this man is blind!

Even if you couldn't see, you have a history of knowing things, even what people are thinking, so surely you would know that this man is blind.

He's blind; he wants to see. Surely you know that!

I'm sure He knew this; however, this story points us toward one profound principle – you have not because you ask not.

I had subconsciously believed that God knows my needs, desires, and pain, and He will just take care of them.

When I read the scriptures, though, I find that I am the one who will have to trigger His move in my life by asking.

> ✈ Look at a statement from the framework for prayer that Jesus gave us called The Lord's prayer.
>
> *Give us this day our daily bread.*
>
> Luke 11:3

> ✈ Look at what Jesus said toward the end of His time on earth…
>
> *In that day you will no longer ask me anything. Very truly I tell you, my Father will give you whatever you ask in my name. Until now you have not asked for anything in my name. Ask and you will receive, and your joy will be complete.*
>
> John 16:23-24 (NIV)

As I think about it, I have struggled with, wondered about, or have needed many things that I had not even mentioned to God (even though He is right with me). #rude

Are you struggling in your role as a parent? Ask Him for help.

Are your finances out of whack? Ask Him to show you what to do.

Do you need to hire a new employee? Ask Him for the right person.

Do you need a buyer for a house you want to sell? Ask Him for one.

Do you need a miracle in your life? Ask Him.

Did you lose your keys? Ask Him to show you where you left them. Yes, He cares about that, too!

Are you worried about ANYTHING? Convert your worries into prayers!

We think about these things all day; we ask friends what they think or for their help, but we neglect the One called our helper.

Wow!

So, bringing this home...

He is right here with me, and He is asking me the same question He asked Bartimaeus.

What do you want me to do for you?

Today, I am committing to ask.

I give up the worry, overwhelm, frustration, confusion, and a helpless feeling, and I simply ask.

And because I know that when I ask according to His Word He answers, I will praise Him like crazy today, too.

What do you think about this verse? What are you going to do differently?

DAY 25

Wait, what?

◆ ◆ ◆

When I started driving, I was a speedster!

I actually believed it was my duty to be ahead of every car around me (don't tell my mom, and no, I no longer drive like that).

One of my dreams was to travel to Germany and drive on the Autobahn, a highway with stretches that have NO speed limits.

They "advise" you to drive under 81 miles an hour, but it is not illegal to go above it.

My thought process was: these cars have such powerful engines, and driving them at 40 miles an hour is such a waste.

Some things have power, and that power has to be kept under control, like cars.

Other things have power, and that power needs to be UNLEASHED, like PRAYER.

Prayer is so powerful, but the power in it is one I need to unleash on my life, family, and destiny.

Did you know that in Bible times, Elijah prayed that it would not rain in Israel, and it didn't?

For three and a half years!

Let's put that into perspective.

If he prayed that prayer today, the next time it would rain would be three years from today! Think about that.

That's the power of one man's prayer.

Now, you might be thinking what I did: "Well, that was Elijah, a mighty prophet of God. Of course his prayers were powerful!"

I think God knew we would believe that, so He had this written in the Bible just for us:

> *Elijah was as human as we are, and yet when he prayed earnestly that no rain would fall, none fell for three and a half years!*
>
> James 1:17 (NLT)

Well, there goes that. Elijah was as human as I am.

And that verse was written right after this one:

> *The earnest (heartfelt, continued) prayer of a righteous man makes tremendous power available [dynamic in its working].*
>
> James 1:16 b (AMPC)

So God says, we can pray powerful prayers, and then uses the example of Elijah's prayer.

Well, I guess I need to start learning and practicing, and that verse gave a lot of pointers, so let's take a look:

The earnest (heartfelt, continued) prayer of a righteous man makes tremendous power available [dynamic in its working].

Heartfelt – My heart needs to be in it. The distracted "Lord-you-know-I'm-late-for-work" prayers, ones that don't move God or me won't cut it.

Continued – needs to be a habit, not an on-and-off thing.

Righteousness – need to pray from this standpoint. Righteousness is a legal term meaning "right standing." Jesus gave us righteousness or right standing when He died on the cross. It is a gift. (2 Corinthians 5:21). We can't pray powerful prayers from a place of guilt and shame, so we must develop faith in the righteousness Jesus died to give us access.

Tremendous power – I have to believe that things happen when I pray, even before I see the answer (Mark 11:24). Why? Because His Word says so!

I may not be able to pray to stop rain for three and half years right now, but I can start practicing these three disciplines that will make my prayer life more and more powerful with each passing day.

Who knows how much more powerful my prayers will be if I do this consistently over the next thirty days? #NewHabitForming

What do you think about this verse? What are you going to do differently?

DAY 26

It's time to wake up!

◆ ◆ ◆

"Don't let him find you sleeping when he arrives without warning, I say to you what I say to everyone: Watch for him!"

Mark 13:36-37 (NLT)

This scripture was written right after the description of what the end times will be like.

The bottom line is, He will arrive without warning, and we should live every day with that in mind.

Now, I had always been told the scary part of Jesus' second coming, so my default was to push that thought to the back of my mind.

The truth is, whether I push it back or keep it in the forefront, He's coming!

I might as well make sure I'm prepared and I watch for Him.

So, if He is coming, what am I supposed to do?

Well, on His way out, Jesus gave His disciples their assignment, and that's our assignment, too.

I mean, it's like we have a test coming, and He literally told us what the questions are.

> *"Then Jesus came to them and said, "All authority in heaven and on earth has been given to me. Therefore go and make disciples of all nations, baptizing them in the name of the Father and of the Son and of the Holy Spirit, and teaching them to obey everything I have commanded you. And surely I am with you always, to the very end of the age."*
>
> Matthew 28:18-20

Me, baptize, teach, or make disciples of people?

Nah, that's for the ministers; I'm "just a Christian"!

That's the thing; there is nothing like "just a Christian."

A Christian is a disciple (Acts 11:26).

A disciple who should be taught to obey everything Jesus commanded, including this final one.

But I don't know how to make disciples of people!

Well, Jesus expects us to, so let's figure it out.

First of all, He said to make disciples and teach them to obey everything He has commanded you.

I used to say things like:

✗ "I don't know enough to teach!"

✗ "I don't know enough scriptures!"

✗ "I'm not a good enough disciple yet!"

Let's just say God was unimpressed by my objections.

His response:

> "Are you my follower?"

> "Have you learned ANYTHING from ME?"

> "Then go and teach others, and as you grow, teach them more!"

So I gulped and said yes.

I took inventory of what I had learned:

- ✅ Being a Christian is the BEST thing that can happen to anyone!
- ✅ To have a consistent prayer life.
- ✅ To meditate on the Word.
- ✅ To give generously to my church and kingdom causes.
- ✅ The power of showing up regularly at church.

I started helping others acquire the same disciplines.

As I learned more, I did more.

Today, I want to give you the same challenge.

Start, restart, or uplevel your discipleship game.

We know Jesus is coming back, or we are going to meet Him. That's inevitable.

We know He will ask us what we did to advance His kingdom on earth with the life He gave us.

We now have time to work on it, so we'll have an answer we're proud of.

Over 200 days ago, I committed not to let my head touch my pillow at night unless my life has impacted another for the kingdom, and by His grace, I've kept it.

You can make the same commitment with me, and on that last day, we'll hear Jesus say to us, "Well done, good and faithful servants!"

What do you think about this verse? What are you going to do differently?

_____

_____

_____

_____

_____

_____

_____

_____

_____

_____

_____

_____

_____

_____

_____

_____

_____

_____

_____

_____

DAY 27

Yaaaasssss!

◆ ◆ ◆

Today, I studied a scripture verse that almost made me do cartwheels! (I'm over 40, no cartwheels for me!)

First, the backstory.

I have dealt with fear all my life. Afraid of failure, rejection, of showing up as the real me, and so on.

In the beginning, I allowed the fears to stop me from taking bold steps.

As I grew in the Lord, I began to understand that fear was Satan's perverted version of faith, and that just like faith, it will attract what I fear into my life.

I started developing my faith, and by that faith, I have done A LOT over the past few years.

I didn't let fear stop me anymore, but I didn't get rid of it either.

Recently, I decided I was done with fear and started my journey to a life without it as a prominent player.

Do you know how many times "Fear not" shows up in the Bible?

114!

(BTW, if you're fearful, this is proof you are not one-of-a-kind or unique. You are not in it alone. God saw that as a problem and addressed it directly over a hundred times!)

If He says "Fear not," then it must be possible to live a life in complete victory over fear.

I mean, there's no way He's the kind of God that would demand of me what I can't do, right?

Anyway, this morning, I meditated on this beauty:

> "Don't be afraid, for I am with you. Don't be discouraged, for I am your God. I will strengthen you and help you. I will hold you up with my victorious right hand."
>
> Isaiah 41:10

Wow!

First of all, my loving Father says, "Don't be afraid."

He is literally saying, "Nneka, don't be afraid; I'm here with you."

Think about anything you are afraid of: life's challenges, heights, Satan, the neighborhood bully who is bigger than you...

Imagine the fear you would feel if you were out riding your bike and said bully cornered you.

You'd be scared spitless, as you should be.

What if, as he walked toward you, your dad showed up?

Your dad who loves you and would do anything to protect you.

Your dad whose 6'5" frame dwarfs the bully.

At that moment, what happens to the fear?

It disappears and boldness replaces it!

You'd probably stand beside your dad and start taunting the bully.

What drove out the fear? Your powerful dad being with you.

God is saying to us today, "Don't be afraid; I am with you!"

He even went on to say in the second part of Isaiah 41:10:

"Don't be discouraged, for I am your God, I will strengthen you and help you."

Again, would He tell me not to be discouraged if it wasn't possible? No!

But why shouldn't I be discouraged?

Because He is my God, and He will help me.

Imagine that!

Imagine a God so powerful that He created the entire universe.

The Bible says His throne is in the heavens, and He rules over all.

That powerful God says He will help me.

What?

♡ If I have that kind of help available, what is there to be afraid of?

♥ If I have that kind of help available, why should I be discouraged?

♥ Could it be that I'm afraid and discouraged because I meditate more on the problem than on the One who is my help?

♥ Could it be because I have more faith in the ability of my circumstances to hurt me than in His ability to help me?

Today, I recommit to banishing fear from my life.

It will require three things (at least):

> Pray for understanding what the Word says about fear. Psalm 119:18

Meditate on the "fear nots" of the Word.

Practice when fear shows up.

NO FEAR HERE!

What do you think about this verse? What are you going to do differently?

DAY 28

You are now certified... by God!

◆ ◆ ◆

Huh?

Give me a moment, and I'll explain.

When I was younger, I was embarrassed by all the mistakes and challenges I had faced: my struggles to maintain a consistent prayer and study life, how socially awkward and how afraid I was to show my authentic self, how terrified I was to be on stage, how I struggled as an entrepreneur, the list goes on.

The thing is, God helped me overcome each of these things to a considerable extent.

Am I still a work in progress? Yes, and I always will be, but I am nowhere near where I used to be.

That is such a wonderful testimony, but it's also a HUGE opportunity.

You see, our testimonies don't end with what God did for us; they MUST translate to how we use our victory in the service of others.

Here, I'll show you:

> Praise be to the God and Father of our Lord Jesus Christ, the Father of compassion and the God of all comfort, who comforts us in all our troubles, so that we can comfort those in any trouble with the comfort we ourselves receive from God.
>
> 2 Corinthians 1:3-4 (NIV)

A few points to note:

- ✅ God is the God of all comfort, and He comforts us in ALL our troubles (as a side note, if you are experiencing any trouble, reach out to Him. He comforts us in ALL).
- ✅ He comforts us SO THAT we can comfort others with the same.

The testimony is not the end; it is proof that you're now certified to comfort others!

What if you took every challenge and converted it into a platform to help others?

Imagine if it was no longer a sore point but a gift that keeps giving to others.

I am passionate about helping people develop strong prayer and study lives because of my struggles.

I help people own who they are and become the best versions of themselves because I was so ashamed of myself and my uniqueness.

I built a business around helping new entrepreneurs THRIVE because I was so clueless.

I teach people to speak confidently and powerfully on stages, whether virtual or in-person, because I struggled with speaking publicly.

I comfort others using the same comfort I have received.

Today, I have a challenge for you!

Take a few minutes, and take an inventory of all the troubles God has helped you with.

Those are the areas where you are certified to help!

Commit to start helping others who are going through the same thing.

You may feel you're not worthy, but the scriptures say otherwise.

Imagine how rich your life will be if you multiply your victories by working with God to reproduce them in the lives of others.

Think of all the lives that will change.

If you start doing this today and stay on it, you will create a life of PROFOUND impact, one beyond your wildest dreams.

What do you think about this verse? What are you going to do differently?

DAY 29

Well, when you say it like that...

◆ ◆ ◆

One of the reasons I love the Bible is that it has the nicest things to say about me.

This is how it describes me:

> But you are a chosen people, a royal priesthood, a holy nation, God's special possession, that you may declare the praises of him who called you out of darkness into his wonderful light.
>
> 1 Peter 2:9 (NIV)

All those descriptions!

Let's unpack them.

I am chosen.

God doesn't have to like me because I am His creation.

He does not have to put up with me because Jesus died for me.

He chose me.

I'm a royal priesthood.

What? Two fantastic words in one phrase.

First of all, I'm royalty.

Now, if I were English royalty, that would be HUGE, but I'm kingdom royalty.

I'm a member of the heavenly royal family, the ruling family of the universe.

Secondly, I'm a priest.

That means I'm a mediator between men and God. I'm an ambassador representing God to people and also representing people to God.

Wow!

I'm part of a holy nation.

Holy in one sense means I live right.

It also means that I am set apart, dedicated, and consecrated to God.

God's special possession.

Now, being God's possession is fantastic enough, but being His SPECIAL possession is a whole other thing.

I'm special!

I'm not ordinary; I'm not a nobody, I'm special to the one who is the most special person in the universe.

That I may declare the praise of Him who called me out of darkness into His wonderful light.

My mission is to show and tell how good God is!

Now I feel all warm and fuzzy.

Today, my commitment is to bask in His love and all He has done for me and spread the word about how good He is.

What do you think about this verse? What are you going to do differently?

DAY 30

I belong to the most important family

◆ ◆ ◆

My friend adopted a beautiful baby boy, Joe, three years ago.

I remember the long process and how we prayed and trusted God for everything to work out.

On the day everything was finalized, her joy was really out of this world.

She was so excited!

She had a room set up, she had picked out the school he would attend, and she set up a college fund for him. She did it all.

Joe did nothing to deserve everything she was doing, she did it all because he was the object of her affection.

Well, look at what God says about you and me:

> God decided in advance to adopt us into
> his own family by bringing us to himself

> through Jesus Christ. This is what he
> wanted to do and it gave him great pleasure!
>
> Ephesians 1:5 (NLT)

Wow!

Decided in advance.

God didn't have to adopt me; He decided to!

He wanted to!

Adopted into His family.

I am a member of a royal family.

Jesus is the king of all kings, which means I was adopted into the ruling power of the universe!

Well, Selah (pause and think about that).

I have been so conscious that I'm a part of the Unachukwu family, but not of the family I was adopted into.

What if I walked around knowing that I am Nneka Unachukwu Christ?

Won't I show up differently?

Won't I believe differently?

It gave Him great pleasure, even more so than my friend, who is now Joe's mom. Adopting me gave God GREAT pleasure.

We've been sold a lie that God is mad at us, but it gave Him GREAT pleasure to add me to His family. He had all these kids, but He wanted ME!

And the best part?

I did nothing to deserve all this; I just happen to be the object of His affection.

#InMyFeelings

Wow!

Today, I'm going to spend time meditating on who I am in Christ.

Imagine what life will be like if we can walk around with this consciousness.

Who wants to meditate on this truth with me today?

DAY 31

You are God's weapon!
A mighty person
in His hands.

◆ ◆ ◆

Now, when I first heard this kind of talk, I turned around, looked back at the person, and asked, "Who, me?"

And the answer was, "Yes, you."

Today, I want to tell you the same thing: you are a mighty vessel of God. Yes, you!

See, God doesn't call the equipped; He equips the called.

He isn't looking for strong, capable, anointed people; He is looking for *willing* people.

Let's take a tour of the scriptures to see if we can find this principle:

****

Israel had a SERIOUS problem called Goliath. Everyone was terrified of him – the king, the well-trained army, the strong men, everyone!

Who did God use to bring the victory?

A WILLING teenage boy who had never even been in the army!

****

Egypt had an impending national problem – a recession was coming.

First of all, they could not interpret what was coming.

Pharaoh had dreamt about it and knew there was a problem, but he didn't know what it was or how to fix it.

Who did God use to solve that national problem?

A WILLING foreigner called Joseph, a prisoner no less, was the one God used to save that nation!

****

When Jesus was done with his mission on earth and was set to leave, He had to commit His entire ministry into the hands of people on earth who would continue the work.

There were prominent, skilled religious leaders called the Pharisees and Sadducees, but Jesus didn't use them.

Who did Jesus trust with spreading His message to the ENTIRE world?

WILLING tax collectors and fishermen. He also used people who doubted him, like Thomas, and who denied Him, like Peter.

****

So, what is my point?

You are God's weapon!

He wants to do mighty things on earth, but He ALWAYS does these mighty things through people.

People just like you!

You may not be as equipped as you think you should be. The great news is that you don't start by being equipped, but by being willing.

Are you willing?

DAY 32

Ouch! God called me out

◆ ◆ ◆

Four years ago, I was privileged to speak at a Women's Conference on how to become a goal crusher.

One of the ultra-successful's habits I challenged them to adopt was reading.

I had a cute slide with pictures of famous entrepreneurs who are big readers, like:

  ✓ Bill Gates, who reads 50 books a year, even though he was worth $90 billion at the time.

  ✓ Mark Cuban, who reads for three hours a day looking for one good idea, even though he was worth $3 billion and owned 150 companies at the time.

I was funny, though – I added my picture to the slide and said, "I've read 52 books this year; I read a book a week!"

And right there, on the stage, the Holy Spirit asked me a question:

"I've written sixty-six books. How many of them have you read?"

Gulp.

I didn't know how many. And I was sure it wasn't a lot.

I was so intentional about reading personal development books, but I wasn't intentional AT ALL about reading THE book that had the most power to change my life.

Right there, on stage, still speaking to the audience, I repented silently.

That day, I started a journey of intentionally reading the scriptures, digging into them, and squeezing the juice out of them.

Has it been easy? No, but is any great habit?

We have to fight for our good habits.

Sometimes, I wonder why He asked me that question.

I think one of the reasons is this:

> *My people are destroyed for lack of knowledge...*
> *Hosea 4:6a KJV*

The interesting thing about this scripture is that the people being destroyed are His people.

I looked up the meaning of the word "destroy," and it's a pretty harsh one.

Synonyms for "destroy" are words like <u>tear down</u>, <u>pull down</u>, <u>ruin</u>, <u>damage</u>, <u>devastate</u>.

Yikes!

He goes on to give the reason why His people are open to destruction – lack of knowledge!

That means the antidote to destruction is *knowledge*.

I used to read the Bible because it was the good, Christian thing to do.

Now, I am on a quest to understand the Word because I really don't care for the alternative, which is destruction.

I want to live a blessed life and be a blessing to the world. (Yes, the whole world. Reading the Bible will make you start thinking like that).

The more I know Him, the better quality of life I have.

The more I know Him, the better I can weather storms.

The more I know Him, the greater impact I can have.

And I want all that!

I am recommitting to being an intentional student of the Word of God, and I would love for you to join me.

What do you think about this verse? What are you going to do differently?

DAY 33

What's important, anyway?

◆ ◆ ◆

Each time I spend some time in the scriptures, I realize I need to spend *more* time.

It is so easy to be deceived.

It is the Information Age, after all; there is so much out there. But we have to be able to filter it by the Word.

I would like to tell you about a friend of mine, Aidan.

He grew up in Europe before moving to the US at the age of 20. While in Europe, he traveled to many countries, and because of that, he speaks twelve languages. Twelve! He gave his life to Christ while at church with his mom at the age of ten. A short while after, he was baptized with the Spirit and spoke in other tongues. His pastor later noticed he had a prophetic gift and started helping him develop it.

After coming to America, he felt called to full-time ministry, and thankfully, he answered the call. He started holding prophetic meetings that God confirmed with miracles and signs.

It turns out he also had a knack for entrepreneurship, so he built businesses on the side. He was a simple man, so he did it not for personal gain per se but to fund kingdom projects. Over the last few years, he sponsored over a hundred missionaries and more recently built a brand-new building for his home church.

I think he's a really impressive Christian!

What do you think?

More importantly, what does God think?

The answer is, it depends.

So first of all, I totally made Aidan up, but I think he's very cool!

I made him up to bring to light the scripture I would like to share with you.

Impressive as all his gifts and feats are, there is one thing God looks at to see if it matters at all.

> In God's eyes, if Aidan speaks many human languages and in tongues but doesn't love others, he is nothing but a noisy gong.
>
> (1 Corinthians 13:1)

> If Aidan has the gift of prophecy and faith that move mountains but doesn't love, he is nothing.
>
> (1 Corinthians 13:2)

> If Aidan gave away everything to the poor but does not love others, he has gained nothing.
>
> (1 Corinthians 13:3)

Does it mean he should not have done any of the great things he accomplished?

No, a thousand times, no. He should most certainly have done it all.

It just means that love is the most important thing, and we MUST live by it.

Well, my made-up friend Aidan was the kindest man ever, and he lived by the law of love.

So yes, God thinks he's pretty cool, too.

Time to look inwards.

We do and have accomplished so many things, but when God looks at us, the number one thing He will be looking for is how we love.

Do I love people?

I am not too quick to say "yes" without looking at God's definition of love because it is VERY different from love as we know it outside the Word.

My husband says it in a funny way — the world defines love as a feeling you've never felt before.

How does God describe love?

Love…

- is patient and kind
- is not jealous, boastful, or proud
- is not rude
- doesn't demand its own way
- is not irritable
- keeps no record of being wronged

- does not rejoice about injustice
- never gives up
- never loses faith
- is always hopeful
- endures through every circumstance

1 Corinthians 13:4-8

So, back to the question — do I love people?

The answer is, I'm working on it.

What do you think about this verse? What are you going to do differently?

_____

_____

_____

_____

_____

_____

_____

_____

_____

_____

_____

_____

_____

_____

_____

_____

About the author

◆ ◆ ◆

Dr. Una is the founder of Meditate to Thrive — an inspirational blog and print devotional.

She is a multi-faceted leader, author, and speaker whose passion is to help others succeed. She has been privileged to teach and coach many to set goals and take action to make their dreams a reality. Gleaning from her own experiences, Dr. Una teaches with compassion and simplifies complicated concepts.

Dr. Una is a pediatrician and has been the CEO of Ivy League Pediatrics, an award-winning private practice, for the last decade. Armed with a depth of experience and wealth of knowledge from running her own practice, she founded EntreMD, a company designed to help physician entrepreneurs build profitable businesses.

In addition to being a serial entrepreneur, Dr. Una also co-pastors Dominion City Church in Norcross, Ga, with her husband, Pastor Steve Unachukwu. She considers being used by God to impact lives as her greatest success. They have been married for 14 years and have four amazing children.

Dr. Una lives by the motto: Die empty. Do all you can to use everything God gave you to serve your generation.

She blogs at www.MeditateToThrive.com